A FORTNIGHT AT THE FRONT

ALBERT—RUINS OF CHURCH, WITH LEANING-OVER FIGURES OF
VIRGIN AND CHILD (*see page* 15)

ALBERT—RUINS OF CHURCH, WITH LEANING—
OVER FIGURES OF VIRGIN AND CHILD.

A FORTNIGHT AT THE FRONT

RT REV H.R. WAKEFIELD

BISHOP OF BIRMINGHAM

COPYRIGHT INFORMATION

A CURE FOR PESSIMISM

Whether any one has the right to make any statement with regard to something which has only been studied for a short time is questionable, and, therefore, I do not pretend to any dogmatic utterance, but I wish simply to state the effect produced upon me by my time abroad. My experience goes from thirty-five yards from the German trenches right back to the most southern and westerly of our bases. Bearing in mind that through the courtesy of Headquarters I have been able to see everything under the most comfortable and time-saving circumstances, it must be admitted that though my view may have been superficial, it certainly was comprehensive. I had the satisfaction of being able to give a kind word and a blessing even where one was asked not to speak too loud in case our enemies should overhear; I held confirmations in several places, and addressed troops, both wounded and strong and hearty, on many occasions.

The first thing which struck me was the great courtesy and consideration of everybody who was concerned with our visit. That the authorities at Headquarters who were working, as I know, both early and late, must have felt that one was a very unnecessary addition to their troubles is, I should fancy, unquestionable; yet not only did they never show it, on the contrary, they worked every day to make our visit easy and delightful. I know that the Lord Mayor of Birmingham, who spent nearly a week with me, feels this as warmly as myself, and it shows the wonderful calm of an Englishman that we were both so kindly treated, though we added in no way to the happiness or usefulness of anybody. What I have said with regard to the Staff at Headquarters applies also to all those who had to do with us at all the various centres.

The next thing which struck me was the way in which the British have, as it were, taken possession of the whole of that area for which our people are responsible. You go through village after village, and the ubiquitous person is our soldier. He appears out of farm buildings, he leans over gates, holding difficult conversation, not only with the young maidens of the village, but with dear old ladies who can be seen taking a motherly interest in him. In the towns he pervades the whole place. Always bright and cheerful, and yet conscious of his responsibility, our khaki-clad young fellow maintains his good character and earns the respect of the people. I asked a

French Archbishop and also a French Bishop, the jurisdiction of both of whom is within our area, if they were satisfied with the behaviour of our men, and on each occasion the answer was that they were beyond reproach. We do not seem to be visitors in France, but we almost appear to have taken root there. The buildings we are putting up, the railway extensions we are making, the way in which we have turned bare spaces into towns, all these things make one feel as if we were permanent institutions and not birds of passage. It is not altogether wonderful that some of the more ignorant French people should say that they do not believe we are ever going away; whilst on the other hand, some French officers told me that their confidence in our alliance had become immensely greater because we had done everything in such a stable manner, one man going so far as to say to me that he considered one of the surest signs of our determination to see this war through was that so many of our officers had taken houses for three years certain. It is only just to add in regard to a large number of the buildings we have put up that they can be taken down, carried away and be put up over here with practically no difficulty. Another impression produced upon me was one of increasing respect for the adaptability of the Englishman. It shows itself in innumerable military ways which I hardly have the right to mention, but one may be permitted the general observation that there is no kind of obstacle which we do not seem to surmount and even sometimes to turn to an advantage. What we have done in turning to good use even some extraordinary effects of shell fire upon buildings made me more than astonished; perhaps I may be allowed one instance. Somewhere in France there was a railway station and near it an estaminet; both, as far as one could judge, were destroyed, with the exception of a portion of a chimney. By some miraculous means which I cannot describe, one went along all kinds of underground places, then up some steps and into what I believe was a portion of the chimney, and from there through a crevice one was able to see a good deal of the German lines quite close by. When one came out again, one could not in the least tell where it was that one had been. To take a less warlike instance of our power of getting over difficulties: a certain officers' mess is established in a French farm which a few months ago had a duck pond which gave forth an odour which was both unpleasant and unsavoury. Consequent, I believe, upon the enthusiasm of a particular major, within four months the pond was empty, the ground was levelled, the seeds were sown, and when I was there the pond had become quite a respectable lawn-tennis ground. It is safe to say that one's gardener would have expected to have four years instead of four months for such an operation.

I may give, perhaps, another instance of this special quality of the Britisher. The Artists' Corps went out to France for ordinary duties; they have now become an Officers' Training Corps, and an enormous percentage of them are holding commissions in every kind of regiment.

Not only so, but they are largely instrumental in carrying on a kind of Sandhurst on French soil; they are, I believe, influential in the management of a bomb school, and last, but not least, they have a band in which the soldiers rejoice, and of which I wish there were many more at the Front.

I am personally greatly indebted to the Artists; first, because a very charming officer of their number was placed in charge of me for a considerable time and bore with me in patience; secondly, because I found such a hearty welcome from them at their mess and so many friends amongst their number; thirdly, because they turned up so well at the Parade Service at which I was the preacher!

The next thing which struck me was the calm in the trenches. Over here in England we seem to live in a continual change of feeling. We get the account of some engagement in which we are successful, and immediately we conclude the war is going to be over tomorrow, and people who are wont to go abroad for a holiday think it is time they went to Messrs. Cook's office to see about their tickets. But on the way they see the placard of an evening paper which tells of some minor disaster to our Forces, and then they return home, they call together the family and they tell them that the future means either the destruction of the country or twenty years of misery and poverty; the bulk of the misfortune, of course, being sure to rest upon their own individual shoulders. It is refreshing to get away from this atmosphere and to go into the trenches where everybody is doing his bit of work, content with somewhat unpleasant circumstances so long as through him England is served. Whenever, in future, I am inclined towards a fit of pessimism, I shall shut my eyes in order to see once again, with the vision of the spirit, a stalwart Britisher of the Worcester Regiment, not very far from the German lines, on a certain afternoon, when a most appalling thunderstorm was raging and some German shells were falling. He was munching the thickest slice of bread and jam that I have ever seen, and looking with a mild contempt at the intruding figure of an unknown padre whom a considerable number of his comrades were greeting because they recognised in him their Bishop. He put down now and again his refreshment in order to do some bit of work, but he was just as calm and collected as if he had been in his Worcestershire village and not in the trenches.

That which carries our men through so many difficulties is another thing which impressed me—namely, their unfailing sense of humour; a humour which is never really hurtful even when exercised upon some one deserving of satire. When he christens a road along which there are a couple of miles of Army Service carts "Lorry Park," when he finds every kind of strange anglicising for Flemish or French words, we know that he is not only having some fun for himself, but also providing amusement for those who come after him. The same humour shines out when he is in hard case. A chaplain told me that he had been addressing informally some wounded men who had just arrived from the trenches. He was expatiating upon the glories of the Victoria Cross because he noticed some of the men came from a regiment one of whose number had recently received that coveted distinction. Suddenly his eloquence was disturbed by a voice proceeding from a man, both of whose feet were swathed in bandages, who remarked, "Never mind the Victoria Cross, give me the Victoria 'Bus!" Obviously the soldier's sense of humour was conquering his pain, and his remark made the rest of the party forget their sufferings for a short time. The only excuse that I can find for the fluctuating feelings of the people at home is the remarkable way in which they minister to Tommy's love of fun. He has every kind of quaint name for the people in "Blighty"—the name which, though derived, I believe, from an Eastern word denoting home, nevertheless expresses something of the attitude noticeable at certain periods, both in people and Press in England, and which appeals through its appropriateness to the humour of our soldiers. But at the same time there is a wonderful thankfulness shown in the face of officers and men when the time arrives for the short spell of leave. The old country and the friends left behind there are, after all, the things closest to the hearts of our men.

The next thing upon which I would comment is the great mutual respect between ourselves and the French. Every time I asked any of our people what they thought of our Allies the answer was one of unhesitating commendation, whilst in the same way when I spoke to French officers or men, they expressed themselves in terms of absolute trust in our nation and her statesmen and soldiers. As one who saw the French during the war of 1870, when—being a boy—I was very susceptible to impressions, I can hardly express the difference I notice between the nation then and now. In the former war there was excitement, impulsiveness, over-confidence, want of ballast; today there is quietude, earnestness, and withal, assurance of eventual victory. More than once I journeyed through a considerable part of the French lines, and I assert with confidence that the Army of France at the present time is incomparably superior to that which she placed in the field in 1870. As to her civilians, I only saw women, children, and old men; I did not, in all my thousand miles of travel, discover a single able-bodied person of military age out of uniform.

The harvest, a very good one, was in full swing. Every family was out in the fields, all doing something towards the in-gathering. I have a picture now before my eyes of seven people, all undoubtedly coming from the same house, working away hard, whilst at the tail end of the procession appeared what might have been the great-grandpapa, no longer capable of bending down for harvesting, but who, nevertheless, had his piece of work in carrying about the baby, who, of course, could not be left behind alone in the house. The whole nation is doing its utmost; can we quite honestly say the same of England?

VERMELLES—THE CASTLE RUINS

Photo : *M. Rol, Paris]*

VERMELLES—THE CASTLE RUINS

Another subject which was constantly commented upon and appreciated at the Front was the thoroughness with which the Germans had done and were doing everything. It was a matter of genuine regret with our people that they could not be as wholehearted as they would wish to be in appreciation of our enemies, in consequence of the way in which they had sullied the fair fame of noble warfare. If there is one thing a soldier wishes to do more than another it is to be able to speak with respect and admiration of his opponent, and, unfortunately, what the German would have gained by his magnificent methodical thoroughness, he has lost through his dishonourable and brutal conduct of the war. At the same time, it should be fairly stated that in the judgment of those to whom I spoke the destruction of churches by our foes has not been so wanton as is sometimes put before us. It was suggested to me that in all probability the church was often destroyed for the same reason as a high chimney, because it formed an excellent observation post.

Before I leave the subject of the men at the Front, one of their constant questions must be noted, which was whether they might expect as much keenness on the part of our civilian population as was being shown by those under arms. "We are doing our bit, but we shall need increased, even greatly increased, assistance; I suppose we can be sure of getting it." Those words still ring in my ears.

WITHIN RANGE OF FIRE

Perhaps it would be of interest to give a little account, without, of course, mentioning names, of the events of one or two days when a visit was paid to the trenches. On one occasion after motoring through towns that are a household word, both at home and with our Allies, towns which have seen the Germans in them and then driven out of them, places where the buildings are practically level with the ground, the limit for vehicular traffic is reached and one goes forward on foot. Soon you reach a cutting in the ground and you begin to walk along a trench. You turn now and again either to right or left, seeing sign-posts telling sometimes in comic language and sometimes only by number the name, as it were, of the underground street; you then rise a little and find yourself walking in the inside of houses so shattered that you cannot tell much about what they originally were until you are told that they formed a street in a little overgrown village of which nothing is left, and the last inhabitant of which was the station-master, who refused to leave though there was neither train, station nor house for himself left, because so long as he remained on the spot he could claim his pay. Forcible measures had at last to be used to secure his departure. Where you are walking you are yourself hidden from the enemy, but are within the range of their fire. You are taken up to an observation post, where one of your companions incautiously takes out a white pocket-handkerchief and is hurriedly told to put it back in his pocket. You come down again and you proceed cautiously along trenches. Now and again shells pass over, and your careful guide looks to see in what direction they are falling, as, though he is quite unconcerned for himself, he knows that he is responsible for the safety of the troublesome visitor. You are told to keep your head down and not to show, for the moment at any rate, any desire to view the landscape. Soldiers are dotted about here and there, all of them ready to give a kindly greeting, and then at last you reach a point where you are told not to speak loudly because practically only a few yards away is the enemy, who, were he to hear conversation, might think it worth while to throw over a hand grenade. What looks like a tiny bit of glass at the end of a short stick is there before you, and you are asked to look into it; when you do the enemies' trenches are visible to you. Beyond an occasional ping against a sandbag, you have heard nothing to note the existence of rifle fire, except that the men you have passed have got these weapons to hand. You tell the men at the advanced posts how proud their country is of them, how thankful you are to have seen them, how you pray that God may bring them back safe to their homes; you get rid of all cigars or cigarettes you may have upon you, wishing that you had thousands more, and then you return home, varying perhaps the route through the communication trenches.

On another occasion our way took us through a town which is absolutely razed to the ground and is still under shell fire. There I saw two soldiers busy with spades, and I asked what kind of fortification they were putting up, to which, with a broad grin, one replied that they were looking for souvenirs. He was kind enough to give me a complete German cartridge case, for which he refused to take any remuneration. Going on a little farther in this town, we went down some steps and found ourselves in an underground club full of soldiers, who were having a hot meal, were reading papers and playing games, everything being presided over by perhaps the most magnetic person I met on my travels, a young Chaplain to the Forces, who would not wish his name to be mentioned, though there is probably no one out at the Front who will not know to whom I refer. When we went from this place towards the more advanced trenches, I was taken along a road which looked perfectly harmless, when suddenly a stalwart Scotchman told my companion and myself that we must get off it at once as it was a favourite target for German Maxims. Never was General more obediently submitted to than was this, I believe, private soldier. It was on this occasion that we had tea in the dug-out of the Colonel, who bears a name distinguished in English naval, military and sporting life. A characteristic of the German trenches which I noticed on this and other occasions, was that their sandbags seemed to be generally white in colour, at any rate in those of the first line. Leaving the trench on this particular day, we had to go through an almost alarming thunderstorm, which in the course of half an hour made a sea of mud of the place which had been quite dry before. It was curious to notice how petty the sound of the guns appeared as compared with the artillery of heaven.

THE INTERIOR OF RHEIMS CATHEDRAL

THE INTERIOR OF RHEIMS CATHEDRAL

Pathetic incidents occur and touching scenes are visible on these journeys to the Front. One looked in the trenches upon little mounds and crosses, marking the resting-places of men who had been hurriedly, but reverently, buried. There they are side by side with their living comrades, who are doing their work whilst their brothers sleep. Dotted all about the country are little cemeteries, which tell of devotion unto death, and which remind one of all the sorrow this war has caused. It is strange to see how religious emblems appear to have been strong against shell. Constantly you would see a church almost totally destroyed and yet the crucifix untouched, and who will ever forget that sight which can be seen for miles around, of the tower which has been almost shattered to pieces and yet the statue of the Virgin and Child, which was near the top of it, though bent over completely at right angles, still remains, as it were blessing and protecting the whole neighbourhood.

This leads to the consideration of the religious condition of our troops as affected, first, by the churches and worshippers of France, and, secondly, by their own experience in this war. More than one mentioned the pleasure felt at the sight of the little wayside shrines which they passed on their march. Others commented upon the large numbers of people they saw flocking to their early communion, and many expressed a hope that permission might be secured for parade services to be held in the naves of the various parish churches during the winter time, when the cold is great and when it is almost impossible to secure any suitable building other than the churches for worship. Negotiations have been going on upon this matter, and some of the French ecclesiastics are not unfavourable, but a difficulty which is prominent to the minds of some of the French Bishops arises out of the recent separation of Church and State. There is a considerable party in France anxious to secure the ecclesiastical buildings for different sects, and even in some cases for secular purposes. It is felt, therefore, that a precedent might be made of a dangerous character were permission to be given to our troops to have services in these sacred buildings. We may, however, be quite confident that those responsible for the spiritual care of our soldiers in France will deal with this whole question wisely and tactfully. It does seem strange that men who are fighting for the liberties and rights of France, and whose religion is, after all, not antagonistic to the faith of the people of that country, may not have the shelter of the less sacred part of a parish church in order to offer up their prayers to Almighty God. It is when one gets face to face with such circumstances as these that the pettiness of religious strife strikes one with force. Is it just possible that out of this great conflict there may arise a stronger desire for religious unity than the world has ever yet known?

What his experience of war is doing for the soldier in regard to religion is remarkable. It would have been possible that the sight of humanity striving to the death and inflicting horrible suffering might have made our young fellows despair of Christianity. They might have argued that it was of no avail to teach the religion of Jesus when no effect was produced upon international conduct; but they have been able to look more deeply into matters and to realise that not Divine intention was at fault, but human refusal to follow true teaching. They have been able to see God through the cloud of smoke raised by shot and shell, and the Presence of the Divine has not been obscured by the horrors of war. Conscious of the seriousness of the work in which they are engaged, feeling every moment the nearness of eternity, our soldiers have in no craven spirit, but with a due remembrance of their relationship to God and to eternity, turned to religion as a stay in the hour of conflict. What struck one very much was the desire for the understanding of a few central truths, and the evident keenness for big dogmatic statements as to great matters. There was some impatience shown when small details were pressed too strongly, and when terms were used familiar to the theologian, but absolutely incomprehensible to a plain, simple, God-fearing officer or private. It sounds almost an impertinence to speak of the devotion of the chaplains at the Front, but I am bound, after having mixed with a large number of them, to express the deep thankfulness one feels to the padre for all that he is doing. The young men who are now for the first time seeing service as clergy associated with troops, are exceptionally fortunate in the leadership they get from the Army chaplains of long standing. There is something about work with the soldier which intensifies the humanity of any one working for his spiritual welfare.

HOPES FOR THE FUTURE

It would neither be right nor in good taste to mention any names of chaplains, but one may instance the kind of work which one saw them doing. I have already referred to the dug-out club in a destroyed town. I may go on to tell of one who on his bicycle, sometimes late at night, would go away from the centre where he was stationed to outlying districts for the purpose of giving lantern lectures to our troops. When last I saw him he was arranging to give this particular entertainment to a number of our Indian wounded. This chaplain was the life and soul of a great parade service held in a square in one of the French towns, where, by his voice and his enthusiasm, he made the whole service go with fervour and effect. I remember how, on this occasion, numbers of French people came up to me and told me that they were certain that this outward acknowledgment by our soldiers of their devotion to God would be helpful to the spirituality of the whole town. The chaplains abroad have to be business men as well as clergy. The arrangements for services and other matters take up a considerable amount of time. At one base there are about thirty places to arrange for every Sunday, and in these thirty places over sixty services are held. It is no light matter for the Senior Chaplain to see that week by week everything is in order. This particular instance is not an isolated one, and is taken simply at random. Now that there is a Bishop as Deputy Chaplain of the Forces in France, everything should go on in a perfectly satisfactory manner and with great advantage to the chaplains themselves.

SPECIMEN OF SERVICE LIST OF ONE OF OUR BASES AT THE FRONT

DIVINE SERVICES—SUNDAY, AUGUST 22, 1915.

H.C.=Holy Communion, P.S.=Parade Service, E.S.=Evening Service.

CHURCH OF ENGLAND.

B. Details.
8 a.m., H.C. in Orderly Room.
10.46 a.m., P.S. in Y.M.C.A. Hut No. 1.

Reinforcement Camps.
6.30 and 7.30 a.m., H.C. in C.A. Hut.
11.30 a.m., P.S. (open air, weather permitting) at Y.M.C.A.
Hut No. 2 for all Divisions.

If Wet.
10 a.m., P.S. (9, 12, 14 Divisions), C.A. Hut.
11 a.m., P.S. (16, 17, 18 Divisions), C.A. Hut.
11.30 a.m., P.S. (19, 20, 37, 61 Divisions) in Y.M.C.A. Hut
No. 2.
7 p.m., E.S., C.A. Hut.

No. 18 General Hospital.
6.30, 8.16, and 11.30 a.m., H.C., Church Tent.
11 a.m., P.S., Church Tent.
6 p.m., E.S., Church Tent.

No. 1 Canadian Hospital.
6 a.m., H.C., Recreation Tent.
8 a.m., H.C., Nurses Tent.
9.16 a.m., P.S., Recreation Tent.

Liverpool Merchants, St. Johns and Allied Forces Hospital.
7 a.m., H.C., Officers Recreation Tent, L.M.M. Hospital.

6.30 p.m., E.S., Officers Recreation Tent, L.M.M. Hospital.
10.30 a.m., P.S., Ward B. 25 in 23 General Hospital.

No. 3 Canadian Hospital.
6.46 a.m., H.C.
10.30 a.m., P.S.
6 p.m., E.S.

22 General Hospital.
6.16 and 7 a.m., H.C.
11.16 a.m., P.S.
6.30 p.m., E.S.

Convalescent Camp and Isolation Hospital.
6.30 and 8.15 a.m., H.C. in Church Tent, 18 General Hospital.
10 a.m., P.S., Tipperary Hut.

Detention Camp.
10.30 a.m., P.S.

Army Service Corps.
6 p.m., Open Air Service.

23 General Hospital.
6.30 a.m., H.C.
10.30 a.m., P.S. in Ward B. 25.
6.30 p.m., E.S. in Ward B. 25.

24 General Hospital.
6.30 and 8 a.m., H.C.
10.45 a.m., P.S. in Y.M.C.A. Hut 1.
5.30 p.m., E.S. in A 35.

26 General Hospital.
7.30 a.m., H.C., in Ward 15.
10.46 a.m., P.S., Y.M.C.A. Hut.
6.30 p.m., E.S. in 23 General Hospital, Ward 25.

Reserve Parks.
No. 32, P.S., 12.16 p.m.
Nos. 10 and 11, E.S., 6.30 p.m.

20 and 25 General Hospital.
6 and 7 a.m., H.C. in Church Hut of No. 20.
12.15 p.m., P.S. in Y.M.C.A. Hut.

Westminster Hospital.
7 a.m., H.C., English Church.
7.30 a.m. and 12 noon, H.C.
11 a.m., P.S.
6.15 p.m., E.S.

No. 2 Canadian Hospital.
7.30 a.m., H.C.
10 a.m., P.S.
7.30 p.m., Ward Service.

PRESBYTERIAN.

Reinforcement Camps.
9.30 a.m., P.S. (15 and 51 Divisions), Y.M.C.A. Hut 2.
10.30 a.m., P.S. (other Divisions), Y.M.C.A. Hut 2.
6.30 p.m., E.S., all Units, Y.M.C.A. Hut 2.

No. 1 Canadian Hospital.
10 a.m., P.S. in Recreation Tent for all Hospitals except
18 General.

Presbyterian and Nonconformists.
11 a.m., P.S., Y.M.C.A. Hut.
6 p.m., E.S., Church Tent, 25 General Hospital.
7.46 p.m., E.S., Y.M.C.A. Hut.

ROMAN CATHOLIC.

For all Reinforcements, Camps and Base Details, etc.
9.30 a.m., P.S. in Parish Church.
6 p.m., E.S. in Parish Church.
9 a.m., P.S. in Ward 25, 23 General Hospital
7.15 a.m., Holy Mass with Communion in Ward B. 25, 23
General Hospital, for all Hospitals except 18 General
and No. 1 Canadian.

No. 1 Canadian Hospital.
10 a.m., P.S. in Officers MOM Tent.

WESLEYAN AND OTHER NONCONFORMISTS.

All Hospitals, Convalescent Camp and Details.
9.30 a.m., P.S., Y.M.C.A. Hut 1, for all Divisions.

11 a.m., P.S. in S.C.A. Hut.
See Presbyterian Notices.
Evening Services in C.A., Y.M.C.A. and S.C.A. Huts.

21

CARE OF OUR MEN

I come now to say a word as to the care given to the bodies of our men. The hospitals from the trenches up to the base are admirable, and the appliances are of the most modern description. I shall not soon forget how in one place I saw for the first time the travelling X-ray caravan. It seemed very strange to be in the hospital whilst the photograph was taken and then to go out in the road and see the machine which did the work. What a convenience this must be in these clearing hospitals can well be imagined. One cannot mention all the splendid stationary and other hospitals over which one was shown by officials with untiring patience and courtesy. The pride which our fellow-citizens from the Dominions beyond the seas take in the fitting up and working of their hospitals is quite extraordinary, and the same spirit animates the private individuals who have their own large institutions in hotels, casinos, and such-like places that they have taken over. I am not sure that I was not more struck with the splendid arrangements made by the Liverpool merchants for our wounded than by anything else of this kind. There is also what one may call a Convalescent Home for the tired soldier, weary in body, in mind and nerve, which, thanks to the man at the head, seems to be very effective. We all know how the strain of the Front tells upon our soldiers, and especially upon the younger men. They come back to this excellent Home by the thousand; they are kept until really restored, and then they go back cheerful and ready for duty. The last thing before they return is a little service in the chapel, which I had the honour on one occasion to take. It was interesting when paying a visit to another hospital to find that it had been formerly a school, and that as the whole building had not been taken over some of the classes were still being held. I intruded into the schoolroom and gave a talk to the young people about the Alliance.

Although I must refrain most reluctantly from saying anything about the great military personages whom I met in France, and with whom I was so greatly impressed, I may perhaps refer to two French persons of distinction, in no way connected with the war, whom I was privileged to meet. First there is that outstanding personality the Mayor of Hazebrouck, Abbé Lemire. He and I were brought together because he is a clerical municipal dignitary and I was the first clergyman who was ever a mayor in this country. He, however, does more than I have ever been able to do, because he is a member of the Chamber of Deputies, and here in England the doors of the House of Commons are still shut against the clergy. Abbé Lemire was formerly a professor of theology in a seminary and was a man of distinction in his Church. However, since the present influence at Rome he has got out with the authorities and is now excommunicated. The ostensible reason given was that he did not ask Rome's permission to sit as a Deputy. As it was only during the last few years that such a request was made, and as he had been in Parliament for several years before that fresh demand, the Abbé declined to submit. The probability is that he was fairly certain that no permission would be granted, because of the liberality of his opinions. One thing certainly was in the eyes of Rome a grave offence on his part. When the Bill dealing with the separation of Church and State was under discussion, he spoke and voted against it, but when it was passed he did not therefore give up his seat and refuse to serve the Republic any longer. He suggested, when the Bill was in Committee, many amendments which would have greatly eased the financial position of the Church, but these were rejected, mainly because Rome would have no compromise. The short-sighted policy which now prevails at the Vatican, and which has been the cause of the vacillation of the Pope on the subject of the war, has in regard to Abbé Lemire turned him into the hero of all the Liberal Church people of France. He is an extraordinarily winning personality, and as we walked through the streets of his city every woman and child and old man had something to say to him. With one he would discuss the imprisonment of a soldier son in Germany; with another the fact that a married daughter had had a bouncing boy who would be, so prophesied the Abbé, a soldier of France in years to come. To another in deep mourning he had a word of comfort to give; until at last I said to him that he appeared to be not only *le maire* but also *le père* of Hazebrouck. He took me round to his house, which is situated close to the church from the altar of which he is repelled by the vicar, and there he introduced me to the only priest in the neighbourhood who is brave enough to be publicly his friend. Such is the man that Rome ostracises and the people idolise.

ABBÉ LEMIRE

ABBÉ LEMIRE

24

One little matter which should endear Abbé Lemire to the English people is the care which he takes himself, and makes his people take, of the graves of our British soldiers. When flowers are placed upon the French dead the Allies from the other side of the Straits of Dover are not neglected. The religion of Christ will never suffer loss so long as such men as the saint just sketched out exist to prove by sacrifice their devotion to their Master.

Another beautiful character is the present Archbishop of Rouen. Carrying well his seventy-six years, thanks in no small measure to the loving care of his secretary, the great dignitary has passed through the recent critical time for his Church, retaining throughout his breadth of view and his sweetness of nature. Turned out of his official residence, he has built himself another, beautifully situated, in the grounds of which may today be seen English doctors and nurses, and even wounded, resting and gaining health. The morning upon which I saw him I had been celebrating the Holy Communion in the chapel of what once was his palace. When I asked him whether he felt any objection to this being done by our English clergy, he answered, "Certainly not." And then, after a moment's thought, he went on: "After all, what does it matter whether one celebrates in one vestment and another in a different one, if at the root of things we are the same? Of course, at the root there must be union of belief." I do not claim that every Archbishop in France would go so far as he does of Rouen, but when sometimes we accuse others of narrowness we must bear in mind, first, that we are guilty very often ourselves, and, secondly, that there are great instances of breadth to be found within the ranks of Rome. I feel, honestly, that out of this war should come a possibility of a better understanding between the various religious bodies, whose men are fighting for the Allies.

Out at the Front all are living for duty. In five hours from London one can be at the very heart of affairs, and yet you are in a different world. One thing, and one only, animates those brothers of ours, so close to us and yet whose spiritual atmosphere seems so different. All the little things are relegated to their proper place; the really important question absorbs every one from the Commander-in-Chief through the whole of the Army. The drop, as it were, from the high standard of headquarters in France to the capital of the Empire depresses a good deal. If only one could make people understand that the whole position is intensely serious, and that the possibility of our Empire in the days to come being influential for the benefit of the world, nay, the possibility of our being a free nation; that these things rest upon our being at home instinct with the same devotion as our people at the Front, we should find that it would be unnecessary to issue almost despairing recruiting bills, and that all would be rushing to service in the cause of God and country, crying, "Here am I, send me."

25

I am tempted after setting down my impressions of my visit to the Front to take a general survey of the countries engaged in the war, two of which I lived in for a considerable time, and all of which, with the exception of Japan, I have visited during my life.

It is natural to turn one's attention first of all to the instigator of the war, Germany. Those of us who know that country are capable of understanding the readiness with which it plunged into the ocean of blood, and the determination with which it has carried on operations. Ever since 1870 Prussia has regarded itself as the Dictator of the Continent of Europe. Although for some ten years after the Franco-German War it was a poor country, it was nevertheless laying the foundations of that preparedness for eventual attack upon others, which it felt would be necessary in order to consolidate its position of prominence. After 1880 the great growth in material prosperity facilitated the extension of armed power, whilst national pride, which before had been reasonable, now grew into an extraordinary conception of the Divine right of Teutonic aspirations. The Prussian was not blind to the fact that his claims would meet with the inevitable opposition of other Continental Powers, but having cowed the minor German States he felt sure of victory, with those States by his side.

I suppose no people really dislike each other more than the Bavarian dislikes the Prussian neighbour, and probably no characters are more antagonistic than those of the Saxon and the Prussian, but under the iron hand of the military despotism of Berlin, Munich and Dresden came to heel. As to Austria, bearing in mind all the probable disputes between its various component parts, so soon as the present Empire passes away, she feels that safety for her lies only with association with Prussia, though here again there is no love lost between the peoples.

Germanic patriotism is aggressive, and there is certainly some excuse, when we bear in mind that there is a constantly growing population and there is not very much room still left uninhabited. Colonial expansion is the special desire of the heart of Germany, and it is here where she comes into conflict with Great Britain, though it must never be forgotten that there is nowhere a German feels happier than in one of our English dominions. Conscious that her colonising power has proved to be very slight, there have been moments when she has been anxious to meet Great Britain for the purpose of securing some dominions beyond the seas in association with ourselves, and I should not be surprised if, when the question of peace is before us, she should suggest a bargain whereby it is made easy for her to expand on other continents, she agreeing to surrender that which she so far holds by temporary conquest in Europe. It is when one reads the Old Testament that one can best understand Germanic patriotism of today. Just as the Jews of old got an inflated idea of the meaning of being the people of God, so is it with Prussia today. She believes herself to be appointed for the management of much of the world, and she thinks that she can be allowed to attain this goal by a most uncivilised war. The German does not love cruelty, but the civilisation of the Prussian is something which is a thin coating over a rather brutal nature. The constant mention of Kultur in German writings has in itself almost proved that it is something only lately put on, and that it fits badly. The Prussian is easily made coarse. He is learned, he is what he calls "gemuethlich," which can be described as kindly disposed. He has an over-elaborated polish which is a clumsy imitation of French politeness. His table manners are slightly improving, but the vice of his capital city is disgusting in its coarseness, and some of the jests he attempts are Rabelaisian, except that they have no humour. His religion is that of the Old Testament, and his preachers are powerful to stir him to warfare, but incapable of instilling into him high principles. His jealousy of England was not unnatural. With a strenuous determination Germany was working earnestly for pre-eminence, and we seemed over here to be comparatively careless and to be lacking in force and in the deepening of character.

It was in the less useful things in our social life that Germany imitated us, because in regard to the greater things the Prussian felt himself to be a more earnest striver than we here were. He was ready to copy our clothes, some of our sports, certain peculiarities of our manner, but he could not, and today he cannot, understand the real centre, as it were, of the English disposition. The Crown Prince is a typical case of a man who anglicises himself in regard to the excrescences upon our national character, but who cannot by any possibility, though he had an English grandmother, ever understand what a Britisher is. He may wear collars and riding breeches which are copied from productions of a Bond Street hosier or tailor, but he will still go on looting, and he will still show by his utter want of nobility of ideal that he is a somewhat decadent specimen of the lower type of Prussian character.

Although Germany meant war on the Continent, it was not until after the Agadir incident and the diplomatic defeat inflicted by England that there was any real dislike of ourselves. After that time there was undoubtedly a belief that sooner or later there would have to be war with Great Britain, or a great general settlement which should prevent the two nations from engaging in strife. Before that time there were always possibilities of disagreement, but there were also means by which the difficulties could be reconciled. It seemed good to bring the various elements in the two nations together. Some tried to associate the merchants, the legal administrators, the journalists of the two countries; I myself took some part in bringing together the clergy and ministers of England and Germany. I suppose we all felt the possibility of disturbance between our two lands, and it was when I became practically certain that the efforts we were making were vain that I became merely a nominal adherent of the excellent associations which were striving to promote union.

The war came and found Germany ready, united, patriotic, with the feeling of "Deutschland ueber Alles," running through the whole of the central Empires and being a very real inspiration. I may take a very low view of some parts of the German character, but as to the determination, the thoroughness and the unyielding devotion to what is believed to be the goal, I cannot but bend my head in the deepest respect. Let no one believe in the suggested breakdown of Germany. There must be an absolute crushing of the despotic ideals which instigated and at the present day carry on the war. The Brandenburg Gate at Berlin will have to be battered down, or at least the Niederwald Monument of the victory of 1870 hurled into the Rhine, before peace will be secured.

Just now the German is a brave, disciplined, determined, brutal foe, led by a Sovereign who knows that this campaign will either place him first of all Earth's monarchs, or disgrace him and his country for all time. He knows also that he must do the work himself, for from his eldest born nothing stable or wholesome is to be expected.

Germany will offer Britain a bargain before this war is over, probably disgraceful to us but tempting in its clauses. It might be summed up, "the land for Germany and the sea for Britain." It is not surprising that up to the present, neutral nations on the Continent believe, or profess to believe, in the victory of Germany. All that they can see is that on the whole success has so far, on the Continent, rested with the central Powers. Sir Edward Grey was absolutely right when he said that the Balkan States, and it probably would be true of Turkey also, would be at the disposal of the Powers towards which victory seemed to incline. Self-interest has to be, unfortunately, the motive inspiring petty States. If it be true that M. Delcassé, the French Foreign Minister, resigned because of his distrust of Greece, no one need be surprised. Greece is in a very difficult position, not only because her Queen is a German Princess, but also because if by any chance Germany were victorious and Greece had taken up arms against her, the German demands upon that small country would be such as would mean practical destruction.

Turning now to France, we realise that her impelling force in this war is a sacred devotion to country. The pathetic mistake made at the beginning of operations of attempting an incursion into Alsace sprang out of the longing to give back to the beloved land the portion which had been torn from her in 1870. To a Frenchman his earth has a deep meaning, his country has an absolute right to his life, a right never disputed and which is acknowledged with the greatest fervour in the hour of gravest danger. There is no doubt that in the early months of the war the oppression of the last campaign was upon the people; they could still, some of them, remember, and all the others had been told of, the terrible experiences undergone five and forty years ago. When once more Germany was overrunning the land there was for a little time a belief in the inevitable victory of the enemy, but very soon France pulled herself together, and she was enabled to do so because the men leading her, and she herself, had developed a greatness which did not show itself in 1870. I look back to the time when I saw French prisoners spit as they passed their own principal leaders, also in the hands of the enemy. I remember in one German town how subaltern prisoners would cross a road in order to avoid saluting men of superior rank in their own army. I can also call to mind a great moral degradation on the part of many French officers. How different it all is today. It seems to me as if Joffre were typical of the new patience which has entered into the French character. At all times the Frenchman has been the best attacker in the world; today he has learnt the duty of patient warfare. When the French Commander-in-Chief says that he is nibbling at the Germans, he is making a statement which would have been impatiently received in the days gone by, but which is, after all, under present conditions not only necessary but the most difficult of warlike methods. Today France is earnest, whilst in 1870 she was only eager. Her moral position has also changed. Behind the armies today woman is present, not to minister to passion but to minister to suffering, and to ennoble in thought.

The salvation of France has been, under God, its motherhood. The relationship between, not only the boy, but the grown man and his mother, has remained upon me as the most beautiful thing in the way of relationship that I have ever known. When I hear that almost invariably the dying soldier in France, of all ranks, speaks as his last word upon earth the one that he first spoke—"Maman," I know that I am being told an absolute truth. It may be that in the past the French character has suffered through passion, but if woman has sometimes been an evil influence, assuredly she has oftener certainly proved herself a blessing to the men of the land.

It is a delight to one who loves France, but who was never quite sure that she was to be trusted in difficult moments, to feel now that she has all the stability which will make her carry on to the end this awful war.

There is another class to which France owes much of her reformation: the religious, the Clergy and the Sisters. It is a pity that at the present time, through harsh dealing, she is deprived of the perfect nursing and caring for, of some of the religious Orders, as one hears rather painful accounts of the conditions in some of the French War Hospitals, but she has her clergy, her priests, who fight and pray and bear no grudge for injustice done to the

29

Church they serve. Whatever we may feel sometimes about the great Roman Catholic religion, we know this, at any rate, that the power of its members is always at its highest in the hour of greatest sacrifice. I have seen some of its priests ministering, themselves wounded and suffering, and I have thanked God that there were such examples of Christlike devotion at this great hour of the world's history. The sacredness of *la patrie* for Frenchmen is a beautiful thing to dwell upon. We are just learning here in England the first lesson of that which is a finished, perfected knowledge to the meanest of French subjects.

Russia.—Here the atmosphere is different. We are in the presence of a nation naturally, often superstitiously, religious and somewhat uneducated. Russia does not make war in a cool and calculating way. The peasant is ignorant even of the causes of the war. His "little father" orders and thenceforth the war becomes a Crusade, a Holy War. The illiterate, religious, patriotic man or woman in Russia knows no such end to warfare except that which comes from the Czar's command. When you turn to the mercantile class you are conscious that all of it which is not German is strongly, almost vehemently anti-Prussian. The language of commerce today is German. French has been left to the aristocracy. In the shops of Moscow, Petrograd and Nijni-Novgorod, German is the universal language. It is idle to dispute the Teutonic influence which exists, but there is also an intensely antagonistic feeling on the part of those who have experienced the competition of the German. The aristocracy of Russia has a loathing of German coarseness and is French in speech and feeling. All the classes in Russia are simple, the word Kultur does not impress them. The art, the music and the stage effects of Russia are very natural, though often most perfectly expressed.

One is tempted to sum up the present Russian position as that of a simple, religious, almost fatalistic people, ready for all things at the order of the man who is their civil and spiritual head. But Russia was not prepared for war last year. Those of us who have seen in Moscow the drilling of even some of the best known regiments were conscious that we were not looking at the finished article. The Cossack is a natural horseman who in some ways has hardly anything to learn, but the infantry need to be modernised. The Russian will not turn his back, and his preparedness will grow each day.

Italy.—One or two words only in regard to this country, as to which I fancy we at home are a little disappointed. Let us not forget that it was by no means easy for Italy to sever herself from Germany, with whom she had been allied for a long time. We must not leave out of account that there had been no close sympathy with France for some years, nor must the impoverished condition of the country be forgotten. It needed some courage and some faith to ignore the continental impression of the power of Germany and to take up arms at all against her. We must be patient with her, because, though she may not be "on fire" for this war, yet she is in earnest, and her love for England is real.

Belgium.—This little land faced the inevitable, the never-dreamt-of, with an army not intended for international warfare, and which had to be strengthened by utterly untrained civilians. Her action was magnificent. She could have had terms, but she scorned them. Belgium did not love England before this war. One may doubt whether she even trusted her, but she does now. Still even here there has always been a pro-German class, well-to-do and influential, which may be said to have dominated the commerce of Antwerp and other leading centres. There has also been some sympathy with Germany on the part of the people living near to the German border, and no doubt the Belgian nation has suffered through this war from the treachery of some of its own people. But the tenacity of this little land is unquestionable, and her King and Queen will go down to posterity as perhaps the two most knightly characters of this war, two people who seem more to fit in with the days of the Round Table than with the age of Zeppelins and Mines.

On turning to our own Empire, we have to confess that the level of earnestness at the beginning of the war was lower than in the case of France, Russia, or Belgium, and, indeed, in some ways lower than that of Germany. We were thrilled for a moment, as it were, by the knowledge that we were taking up arms because honour demanded that we should, but the public heart was not greatly stirred. Gradually we began to realise that we were engaged in a struggle for our own existence, but even now there are millions in Great Britain who are not persuaded of this fact. Canada, Australia, New Zealand seem to have understood, before the Motherland, how serious the war was for the Empire. It is not for me to declare to Britain her duty; I do not suggest that I know more of the mind of the nation or of the needs of the nation than any other Briton. I think that I may have had greater opportunity of feeling the pulse of other lands than many people, but all of us here at home can see now what our own duty is, and that whilst the usual mistakes have been made, there is now an awakened Empire which dare not in the sight of God refuse any sacrifice in order to crush for at least the generation that is coming, the accursed ideals which the military party in Germany wishes to see dominating the world. Upon this subject the Church must continue to speak and to act; her words being stronger and her actions firmer than up to the present they have been. This war is in my judgment a fight between right and wrong, between God and evil.

Had I my way I would relegate to obscurity for at any rate the whole period of the war every religious division; I would on this all-important matter fall gladly into line with all sides of Christianity in order that men should know that in our judgment the followers of Jesus cannot understand their Leader without being ready to give, if needs be, life, to prevent the victory of wickedness. This is my reasoned judgment, more than ever impressed upon me by my visit to the Front. If we all face the future with this conviction pessimism will die, not to be superseded by a stupid, unreflecting optimism, but by an unremitting devotion, which shall spring out of that courage which belongs to the man who knows his cause is that of God, and that he himself can and must do something towards hastening the triumph which is inevitable if only we are worthy. The religious England to which I look forward is one which has been taught by the awakening of the spirit of Christian patriotism, that in life the beginning and the end of perfection, for nation as well as individual, is the willing offering of body, mind, and spirit in order that it shall be easy for humanity to be free and for right to triumph over evil. May it be our Empire's glory to have the grandest share in this great offering.

www.ingramcontent.com/pod-product-compliance
Lightning Source LLC
Chambersburg PA
CBHW011750020426
42331CB00014B/3350